Citizen Scientist

STUDYING
INSECTS

IZZI HOWELL

T-465-804

Bromley Libraries

30128 80443 056 2

First published in Great Britain in 2020 by Wayland

Copyright © Hodder and Stoughton Limited, 2020

Produced for Wayland by
White-Thomson Publishing Ltd
www.wtpub.co.uk

All rights reserved.

Series Editor: Izzi Howell
Series Designer: Rocket Design (East Anglia) Ltd

ISBN: 978 1 5263 1227 3 (HB)
ISBN: 978 1 5263 1226 6 (PB)

10 9 8 7 6 5 4 3 2 1

MIX
Paper from
responsible sources
FSC® C104740

Wayland
An imprint of
Hachette Children's Group
Part of Hodder & Stoughton
Carmelite House
50 Victoria Embankment
London EC4Y 0DZ

An Hachette UK Company
www.hachette.co.uk
www.hachettechildrens.co.uk

Printed in China

WARNING
TRY TO AVOID TOUCHING INSECTS.
YOU MAY HARM THEM OR THEY MIGHT HURT YOU!

Picture acknowledgements:
Getty: Jirafic 7c, MicrovOne 7b, SimeonVD 14b, jsnyderdesign 15b, mervin07 20, artloct 29b; Shutterstock: penguin_house, designer_an, Magicleaf, vectorOK and Lyudmyla Kharlamova cover, Magicleaf title page, Spreadthesign 4, Elegant Solution 5t, sun7 and Huseyin Altinel 5b, Drogatnev and Maquiladora 6, Elegant Solution 7t, bellflower 8t, BagirovVasif 8b, Kazakova Maryia 9t, Shanvood 9b and 30, LuckyVector 10tl, Vasenina Daria 10tr, Yes - Royalty Free 10bl, Sulee_R 10br, suesse 11, Krissadakorn, Ain Mikail, Cidonia, SLKi and mayrum 12, VectorSun 14t, Studio Photo MH 14c, Jamesbin 15t, Fancy Tapis 16t, Gallinago_media, Silbervogel, RedlineVector, Marie Appert, nikiteev_konstantin and KRIBOX 16b, CloudyStock 17t, Formyline 17c, Artem Twin 17b and 18, NPavelN 21t, Kazakova Maryia 21b, yukitama, HappyPictures, nexus 7, Iamnee, Spreadthesign, Celana, Nikulina Helen A, Foxyliam, Andrey Vyrypaev and Kazakova Maryia 23t, Park Ji Sun 23b, Hennadii H 24t, Iantapix and Pogaryts'kyy 24b, HappyPictures 25t, Tatyana Pogorelova and burbura 25b, Sabuhi Novruzov, Gnatuyk Lesya, Everilda, Kotkoa, Tatiana Liubimova, ArtDemidova and Kunturtle 26, Timofey Tarakanov 27t, pic0bird 27b, mapush 28, Doloves 29t.

All design elements from Shutterstock.

Every effort has been made to clear copyright. Should there be any inadvertent omission, please apply to the publisher for rectification.

The website addresses (URLs) included in this book were valid at the time of going to press. However, it is possible that contents or addresses may have changed since the publication of this book. No responsibility for any such changes can be accepted by either the author or the publisher.

CONTENTS

CITIZEN SCIENCE AND INSECTS

Citizen science is a way to help out with scientific research across the world, by taking part in observations and submitting data. Working as citizen scientists, we can observe insects to see how they live and how we can protect their habitats.

True insects are small invertebrates (animals without a backbone), such as bees and butterflies.

TRUE INSECTS HAVE ...

A segmented body
Insect bodies have three parts – the head, the thorax and the abdomen.

Wings
Insects have one or two pairs of wings, but they are sometimes hidden.

Antennae
These are sense organs that insects use to smell and feel.

A hard exoskeleton
This is a protective layer that insects have on the outside of the body, rather than an internal skeleton like mammals and birds.

Compound eyes
This is like lots of smaller eyes joined into one eye. All insects with eyes have compound eyes.

Six jointed legs
Insect legs are connected to the thorax. Some insects have specially adapted legs that help them to jump or dig.

TYPES OF INSECT

Dragonflies and damselflies
Both species are similar, with a long, thin body. They have two pairs of transparent wings.

Bees, wasps and ants
Many of these species can sting if attacked. Bees and wasps have yellow stripes to warn predators that they sting. They have a narrow waist.

Beetles
Beetles have two pairs of wings – the front pair is hardened and covers the back of the beetle. The back wings are used for flying, and remain folded under the front wings when not in use.

Crickets and grasshoppers
They use their powerful back legs for jumping. They only eat plants.

Flies
Flies fly with one pair of wings. They also have a small set of wing-like structures that they use for balance. They usually have a mouth for biting and sucking.

Butterflies and moths
Butterflies tend to have brighter colours than moths. Butterflies are active during the day, while moths are often nocturnal. They both eat through a proboscis – a long tube used for sucking.

MINIBEASTS

We often use the word 'insect' to describe animals that aren't technically insects, such as snails and spiders. These animals are small invertebrates, but they don't have the right body type or number of legs to be true insects. We can use the word 'minibeast' to describe these animals instead.

minibeasts

Around **1 MILLION** different species of insect have been identified so far, and scientists are discovering more all the time.

5

INSECT OR NOT?

Track down minibeasts in your local area. Use observation containers to get a closer look at their incredible bodies and decide whether or not they are true insects!

This project can be done almost anywhere, from a school playground or a park, to a forest or a pedestrian area. Explore your surroundings until you find a minibeast. Catch it in a plastic insect observation container or a glass jar with a lid.

YOU WILL NEED:

Paper

A pen

A jar

//// BE CAREFUL ////

BE VERY CAREFUL NOT TO HURT THE ANIMAL WHILE PLACING IT IN THE CONTAINER. IF THE MINIBEAST FLIES, LET IT FLY IN. IF IT WALKS, PLACE THE CONTAINER NEARBY AND ENCOURAGE IT TO WALK IN, OR SCOOP IT IN GENTLY WITH A LEAF. TRY TO AVOID TOUCHING IT IF POSSIBLE.

Observe the minibeast inside the container. Take note of the number of legs and body segments, the size and shape of its wings and any other important details. Write down your observations and follow the checklist below to decide if it's a true insect or not.

Minibeast	Observations	True insect?	
Ladybird	Round body	Yes	
	Three body segments		
	Six legs		
	Hidden wings		
	Red with black spots		
Woodlouse	Grey, segmented exoskeleton	No	
	Seven pairs of legs		
	Antennae		
Mosquito	Slim body	Yes	
	Three body segments		
	Six legs		
	Long antennae		
	Proboscis		

INSECT CHECKLIST

Does it have six legs?
Does it have wings?
Does it have three segments?

If your minibeast ticks off all of these points, it's a true insect! If not, it's a different type of invertebrate.

When you have finished, release your minibeast where you found it. Repeat with several other types of minibeast.

GET INVOLVED!

Use an insect identification guide to work out the exact species you have found, rather than just 'fly' or 'beetle'. If you find any minibeasts that aren't insects, try to find out the scientific name of the group that they do belong to.

HABITATS

Insects and minibeasts can be found everywhere – on plants, in soil and in water. They are even found in places we'd rather not find them, such as inside our homes.

MICROHABITATS

Insects and minibeasts can be found in many different specific locations within a habitat. These locations are known as microhabitats. Microhabitats include on flowers, on walls and under stones.

HIDING AWAY

Insects and minibeasts, such as beetles and centipedes, like to hide away in dark, damp places, including under logs and dead leaves. They eat the decomposing remains of plants. This plays an important role in the ecosystem, as insects and minibeasts help to clear and recycle this matter away and stop it from building up.

WARM SPOTS

Insects are cold blooded, which means they can't control their body temperature. They depend on their surroundings to warm up or cool down. For this reason, insects sometimes rest in warm spots on walls, windowsills or fences to raise their body temperature.

Water insects

Many insects can be found in and around fresh water. The young of some insects, such as dragonflies and mosquitoes, hatch and live in water. Adult dragonflies often live near water as well. Pond skaters can balance on the surface of water, while diving beetles dive deep to find prey such as other water insects, tadpoles and even small fish.

At home

Spiders, mosquitoes and flies are all often found in buildings. Mosquitoes gather in homes. Females bite humans to get nutrients from their blood to produce eggs. Flies land on food and can spread germs. Spiders are very common in buildings. They feed on other minibeasts, such as flies, so they keep your home free of other pests.

Fleas live on cats and dogs and drink their blood. Fleas don't live on humans, but they will bite them if they are hungry.

HABITAT HUNTING

Explore your local area and discover the insects and minibeasts that live in different microhabitats.

Choose three different microhabitats (look back on pages 8–9 for inspiration). They could be on a plant, under dead leaves, on a wall or inside your home.

Spend ten minutes examining each microhabitat for the species that live there. Use an identification guide to help you identify any unknown species.

Keep a tally of the different species you spot in each microhabitat and draw a table to present your data. Then, use the Excel program to present your data as a bar chart.

UNDER DEAD LEAVES

Species	Number
Woodlouse	11
Centipede	1
Ant	4
Earwig	1
Ground beetle	1

First, copy your data for each habitat into a spreadsheet in Excel. It should look something like this.

Then, select all of the cells that contain data and click the 'Charts' button. Choose the 'Bar' option. This will create a bar chart from your data.

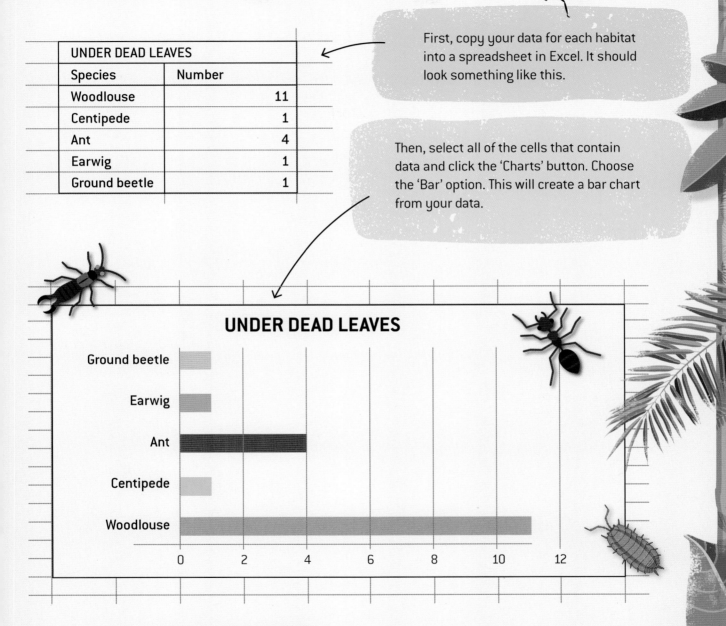

UNDER DEAD LEAVES

GET INVOLVED!

You can upload your research to an online minibeast count, such as www.opalexplorenature.org/bugscount. Other scientists can use your data in their research so that they have more evidence.

MAKE A HABITAT CHOICE CHAMBER

Use choice chambers to find out what kind of conditions woodlice prefer. Each choice chamber is divided into two different conditions — dark or light, or damp or dry. The part that the woodlice move into is the part they prefer.

Before you begin your experiment, make a prediction. Which conditions do you think woodlice will prefer? Use any information that you already know about woodlice to make your prediction. Use the Habitat Hunting activity (see pages 10–11) to track down woodlice.

YOU WILL NEED:

A collection pot with a lid, such as a jar

Soil and dead leaves

5–10 woodlice

2 clear containers with clear lids

Kitchen roll

Black paper

Scissors

Tape

//// WARNING ////
BE CAREFUL HANDLING SCISSORS!

Place some soil and dead leaves in your collection pot to keep the woodlice happy while they are being transported. Collect 5–10 woodlice in the collection pot by allowing them to walk in, or gently scooping them in with a leaf.

Prepare your first choice chamber by dampening a piece of kitchen roll and placing it in half of one of the containers. Fold it if necessary to make it fit. Add your woodlice to the container and close the lid. Leave for 5 minutes. Check back and see which side of the container the woodlice are gathered in – damp or dry? Make a note of your results.

Prepare your second choice chamber. Take the lid of the second container and cut a piece of black paper to cover half of it. Stick the paper to the lid with tape. Repeat your experiment, placing the woodlice in the container, closing the lid and leaving for 5 minutes. Check back to see where the woodlice are – on the dark side or the light side? Make a note of your results.

When you've finished your experiment, place the woodlice back in the collection pot and release them where you found them. Then, look back at your results and think about what they show you. Was your prediction correct?

TRY IT!

Repeat the experiment with some other minibeasts. Are the results the same? You could also change the conditions, such as using two different kinds of soil or leaves. But make sure you don't test any conditions that would hurt the minibeasts.

LIVING TOGETHER

Some species of bees, wasps and ants are social and live together in colonies. Each insect has its own role within the colony.

NESTS

Social insects live together in nests. Ants nest in underground tunnels or in trees. Bees also build their nests in trees or in caves. We encourage bee colonies to nest in manmade hives so that we can collect their honey.

90%

of bees don't live in colonies. They are solitary and live on their own.

REPRODUCTION

The queen is the largest female and the most important insect in the colony. She is mother to most of the colony, as only she can reproduce. Her only job is to lay eggs. New insects for the colony will hatch from these eggs.

queen

drone (male bee)

worker

WORKERS

The workers in a colony perform special tasks, such as finding food, repairing the nest or feeding young. Some worker ants are responsible for defending the nest. They are known as soldier ants and are usually female.

COMMUNICATION

Social insects need to communicate with each other so that they know what's going on in the nest. Honey bees communicate through dance. Ants touch antennae to recognise each other through scent. They also leave scent trails to and from food sources so that other ants can follow them.

worker ant
collecting food

queen ant laying eggs

ant larvae

FOOD WEBS

We use food webs to show where plants and animals get their energy from in an ecosystem. Plants use energy from the Sun to make their own food. Animals eat plants or other animals for food.

PREDATORS AND PREY

Predators are animals that eat other animals for food. The animals that they eat are called prey. Insects are often the prey of larger animals.

predator →   ← prey

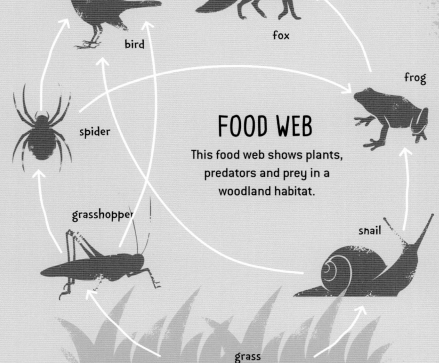

bird

fox

spider

frog

FOOD WEB

This food web shows plants, predators and prey in a woodland habitat.

grasshopper

snail

grass

POPULATION CHANGES

If the population of one part of the food web changes, it affects the other species in the ecosystem. For example, snails and grasshoppers both eat grass. If the snail population increases, there will be less grass for the grasshoppers. Some grasshoppers will starve and die. Other species further up the food web that depend on grasshoppers for food, such as spiders, will struggle to find food as a result.

INVASIVE SPECIES

Food webs are also affected by new, invasive species that settle in an ecosystem. Sometimes, invasive species are introduced on purpose, but they can also be brought to a country by mistake or migrate naturally.

HARLEQUIN LADYBIRDS

Invasive Harlequin ladybirds have been affecting ladybird populations around the world. They are originally from Asia, but were introduced deliberately to Europe and the USA to eat aphids that damaged crops. They were accidentally imported into the UK on plants from mainland Europe.

COMPETITION

The arrival of invasive species means less food to go around. Harlequin ladybirds feed on the aphids that native ladybirds depended on. They also act as new predators in the ecosystem, eating the larvae of other ladybirds. Native ladybird populations have decreased since the arrival of Harlequin ladybirds.

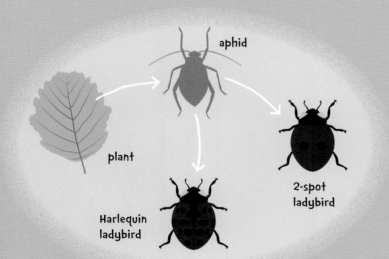

aphid

plant

2-spot
ladybird

Harlequin
ladybird

2004

Decrease in population of the native 2-spot ladybird since the arrival of the Harlequin ladybird in the UK in 2004

44%

TODAY

LOOKING FOR LADYBIRDS

Go on a ladybird hunt and count how many different species you can spot! Are there still native ladybirds in your local area or have invasive species taken over?

Go to a park, garden or woodland area. It's best to do this project in spring or summer as many ladybirds hibernate. Ladybirds are often found on green, leafy plants and trees, but have a look in as many areas as possible. You might want to use a magnifying glass if you have one.

2-spot ladybird

7-spot ladybird

Harlequin ladybird

14-spot ladybird

pine ladybird

orange ladybird

convergent ladybird

9-spot ladybird

When you find a ladybird, identify it using this guide. If you're not sure which type of ladybird it is, check in a book or look online. Draw a picture or take a photo to help you remember what it looks like.

Draw a table to keep track of the number of each species of ladybird that you find. Then, use the Excel program to present your data in a circular pie chart. Each species represents a different section of the pie.

Species	Number seen
2-spot ladybird	2
7-spot ladybird	3
Harlequin	5
Pine ladybird	1
14-spot ladybird	1

First, copy your data into a spreadsheet in Excel. It should look something like this.

Then, select all of the cells that contain data and click the 'Charts' button. Choose the 'Pie' option. This will create a pie chart from your data.

Number of ladybirds seen

- 2-spot ladybird
- 7-spot ladybird
- Harlequin
- Pine ladybird
- 14-spot ladybird

GET INVOLVED!

People across the world are hunting for ladybirds to see which species are the most common. Add your data to the survey at www.ladybird-survey.org/default.aspx or www.lostladybug.org.

LIFE CYCLES

All insects hatch from eggs. After that, different types of insects go through different life cycles.

METAMORPHOSIS

Some insects go through a stage called metamorphosis in their life cycle. Their body is totally rebuilt, rather than growing larger bit by bit. This happens to insects such as butterflies, bees, ants and wasps.

Butterflies lay eggs on leaves. Caterpillars hatch from the eggs.

1

After about 10 days, the butterfly is ready to hatch from the chrysalis. The chrysalis breaks apart and the butterfly flies away.

5

EGG TO BUTTERFLY

This is the life cycle of a butterfly.

2

The caterpillar grows for a few weeks, shedding its skin several times to allow it to grow larger.

The caterpillar goes through metamorphosis inside the chrysalis. Its body breaks down entirely and then reforms as a butterfly.

4

3

The caterpillar attaches itself to a plant and sheds its skin, revealing a tough shell called a chrysalis.

Caterpillars

Caterpillars have to eat a lot of plants so that they have enough energy to go through metamorphosis. However, they can't fly, so it is easy for predators to find and eat them. Caterpillars use different strategies to avoid being eaten, including green or brown camouflage to blend in with plants, releasing substances that smell bad, or being brightly coloured, as this warns predators that they might be poisonous.

Changing shape

Some insects, such as grasshoppers, crickets and dragonflies, don't form a chrysalis to go through full metamorphosis. Instead, they shed their skin as they grow, which is called incomplete metamorphosis. Each time they lose their skin, they change shape a little bit and develop adult features, such as wings.

Egg to dragonfly

Young dragonfly larvae hatch in the water. They live for several years (most of their lives) in the water, where they are known as nymphs. They come out of the water when they are ready to shed their skin and take their adult form with wings to fly.

recently-hatched
dragonfly

adult dragonfly

eggs

dragonfly larva
(nymph)

TRACK A BUTTERFLY LIFE CYCLE

Insect life cycles are going on all around you, but you may never have noticed! Track the life cycle of butterflies and create a fact file to record information about eggs, caterpillars, chrysalises and butterflies. It's best to do this research in spring or summer, when butterflies are most active.

Start by making your fact file. Divide an A4 piece of paper into 4 sections, one for each stage in a butterfly's life cycle. This is where you'll record all of your observations.

///// WARNING /////

DO NOT DISTURB OR TOUCH ANY EGGS, CATERPILLARS, CHRYSALISES OR BUTTERFLIES THAT YOU FIND.

Egg	Caterpillar
Where? When? Which species? Draw a picture	Where? When? Which species? Draw a picture
Chrysalis	Butterfly
Where? When? Which species? Draw a picture	Where? When? Which species? Draw a picture

Different butterfly species lay their eggs on different types of plant. Their caterpillars eat this plant once they have hatched. Look closely as butterfly eggs are small and can be quite hard to spot.

cabbage white on plants in the cabbage family

comma butterfly on nettles and some types of tree, such as elms and willows

monarch on milkweed plants

swallowtail butterfly on plants in the carrot family

peacock butterfly on stinging nettles

Once you've found butterfly eggs, finding caterpillars will be easy as most stay on or around the plant that they hatch on. Take note of where you found the eggs and check back over the next days and weeks until you spot caterpillars.

Around two weeks after you spot the caterpillars, they'll start forming their chrysalises. These can be tricky to spot – look around the plants where the caterpillars live, and under branches and leaves. Be very careful not to damage any chrysalises or knock them off the plant.

Many butterflies are colourful and eye-catching, so they should be easy to spot! Look near flowering plants for butterflies drinking nectar or butterflies laying eggs on plants. If you spot a butterfly laying eggs, make a note of the location and track the life cycle of its young.

GET INVOLVED!

Share your research with other people by uploading the butterflies that you spot to the Big Butterfly Count at www.bigbutterflycount.org (UK) or the Butterflies and Moths of North America project at www.butterfliesandmoths.org (USA).

INSECTS AT RISK

Insect populations are under threat because of human activity. Although they are small, insects are a very important part of natural ecosystems. Losing them has a serious effect on the entire natural world.

Pesticides

Insects can have a negative impact on farms, as they eat and damage crops. Many farmers use pesticides to kill insects and protect their crops. However, pesticides kill any nearby insects, not just those that eat the crops. Organic farmers grow crops without the use of pesticides, which is much better for insect populations.

Habitat loss

Many wild insect habitats are being cleared so that new homes, businesses and roads can be built on the land. When people 'clean up' wild areas, through processes such as deforestation, it destroys important insect microhabitats, such as old logs and wild flowers. People may plant new plants in these areas that don't provide the food and shelter that insects need.

Climate change

Global warming is increasing the average temperature on Earth and affecting weather patterns. This means that plants are flowering and producing fruit earlier than normal. Insects that depend on pollen and nectar go hungry and can die later in the season, as flowers and fruit disappear too soon.

Pollination

Decreasing insect populations puts crops at risk. Insects pollinate plants when they land on flowers to drink nectar. Without insects pollinating these plants, flowers would not be fertilised and no fruit or seeds would develop. This would affect many crops that we grow for food, as well as wild plants, disrupting entire ecosystems.

90%
of the food eaten around the world comes from plants pollinated by bees.

PLANT A BEE-FRIENDLY GARDEN

Some bee species are disappearing because their food sources, such as wildflowers, are being destroyed. Help the bees by planting a bee-friendly garden and track which bees it attracts!

Different species flower at different times, providing food for bees throughout the year.

Spring
apple blossom, crocus

Summer
chive flowers, lavender

Autumn
sage flowers, honeysuckle

Winter
aconite, snowdrops

Find a space for your bee-friendly plants. It could be your school playground, a garden or a balcony. If you don't have space to plant anything, you could look for places where these plants already grow and track the bees that visit them.

Try to plant one bee-friendly plant for every season. Follow the instructions on the seed or bulb packet. You may need to plant them at different times throughout the year.

When the plant is flowering, observe it for 10 minutes. Count how many bees visit and keep a tally. Which flowers are the most popular with bees? Do any other insects, such as butterflies, visit these flowers?

Test your observational skills by using an insect observation guide to work out the species of bee you spot. Count how many of each bee species visit the flower. Are some flowers more popular with some species than others?

TRY IT!

Try planting other species of flowering plant. Are these species popular with bees or other species of insect? Bees also need water to drink, so keep a bowl of rainwater near your plants.

KEEP IT FAIR

All of the experiments in this book will help you to learn more about insects in your local area and how to keep them safe. However, it's important for you to make your experiments fair. If you don't control the different elements of an experiment, the results won't be accurate.

To change	To stay the same
The location	The duration of time
	The time of year
	The time of day
	The amount of noise/disruption you make

VARIABLES

There are lots of elements in experiments. These are called the variables. To make an experiment a fair test, you can only change one variable. All other variables have to stay the same. For example, in the habitat project on pages 10–11, the only variable you are changing is the location. Everything else should stay the same.

INACCURATE RESULTS

If you have more than one variable, you won't know which one has affected your results. For example, if you visited some habitats in summer and some in winter, you wouldn't know if the number of insects was because of the habitat or because of the season. This makes your research invalid.

PLAN AHEAD

It's important to plan how you will make your experiment fair before you begin. This helps to keep the variables the same throughout. Write down important details, such as lengths of time, so that you don't forget.

OVER TO YOU!

When you've finished the projects in this book, why not make up your own?

First, you need to think of an idea that you want to test. This is called the hypothesis. For example,

'I THINK THAT SMALL INSECTS PREFER TO VISIT SMALL FLOWERS.'

Next, think about your variables – what will you keep the same and what will you change?

Then, carry out your experiment. You should repeat it a few times to make sure that your results aren't a one-off. Present your ideas using one of the graphs from the book. Finally, use your results to come up with a conclusion – what do the results show you? Was your hypothesis right or wrong?

GLOSSARY

antennae long, thin sense organs found on the head of an insect

camouflage having a colour or pattern that is similar to the surroundings so it is difficult to see

chrysalis the stage of development of a moth or butterfly in which the animal changes form inside a hard shell

colony a group of the same species of animals that live together

conclusion the opinion you have after finding out all of the information necessary

decompose to break down

deforestation cutting down all the trees in an area

ecosystem all the living things in an area

exoskeleton a hard outer layer that supports and protects the body of an invertebrate

hypothesis an idea that needs to be tested

invertebrate an animal without a backbone, such as an insect, crab or worm

larva the young of an insect that has not yet reached its adult form

metamorphosis the process in which insect larvae transform into their adult form

microhabitat a small habitat, such as the bark of a tree, found within a larger habitat

nymph a dragonfly or damselfly larva

pesticide a chemical used to kill unwanted animals or plants

pollinate to transfer pollen from one part of a plant to another, which fertilises the flower

predator an animal that kills and eats other animals

prey an animal that is hunted and killed by other animals

proboscis a long tube that butterflies use for sucking

species a group of animals or plants with the same characteristics

tally a running total

variable an element in an experiment that can change

FURTHER INFORMATION

BOOKS

Insects and Spiders
Visual Explorers
by Toby Reynolds and Paul Calver
Franklin Watts, 2019

Nature Detective
British Insects
by Victoria Munson
Wayland, 2018

The Great Nature Hunt
Minibeasts
by Cath Senker
Franklin Watts, 2019

WEBSITES

www.natgeokids.com/uk/discover/animals/insects/15-facts-about-bug
Discover some amazing facts about insects and minibeasts.

thekidshouldseethis.com/post/a-ladybug-ladybird-life-cycle-time-laps
Watch a time-lapse video of the life cycle of a ladybird.

www.ducksters.com/animals/bugs.php
Learn more about insects and spiders.

INDEX